# CAMBODIA

*…in Pictures*

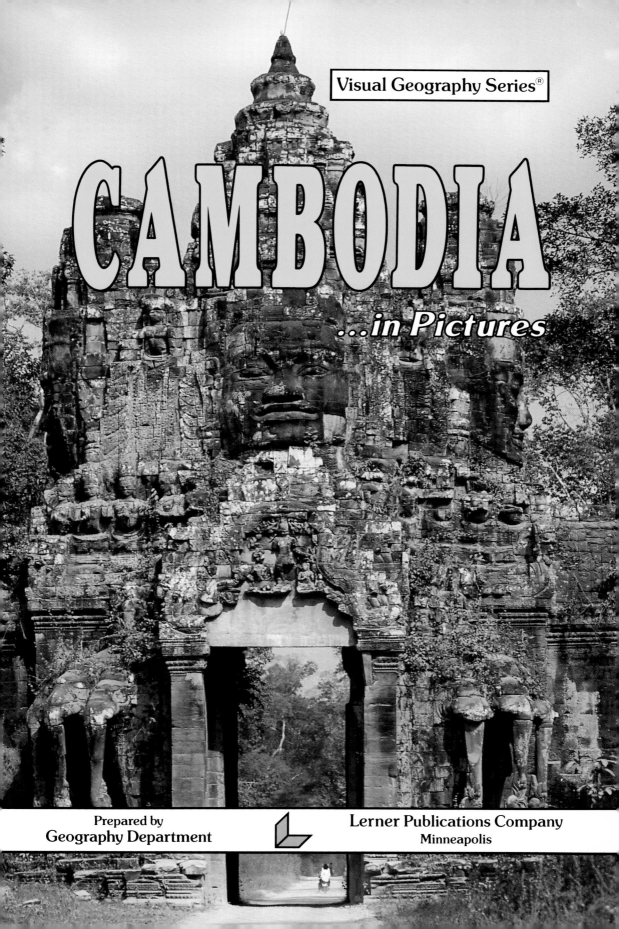

Visual Geography Series®

# CAMBODIA

## ...in Pictures

Prepared by
**Geography Department**

**Lerner Publications Company**
Minneapolis

Photo © Isabella Tree/Hutchison Library

**Buddhist monks ride through Phnom Penh—Cambodia's capital city—on a motorbike.**

This book is a newly commissioned title in the Visual Geography Series. The text is set in 10/12 Century Textbook.

LIBRARY OF CONGRESS CATALOGING-IN-PUBLICATION DATA

**Cambodia in pictures** / prepared by Geography Department, Lerner Publications Company.
  p. cm. — (Visual geography series)
  Includes index.
  Summary: Introduces the land, history, government, people, and economy of a country in Southeast Asia that has been inhabited at least 6,000 years.
  ISBN 0-8225-1905-4 (lib. bdg. : alk. paper)
  1. Cambodia. [1. Cambodia.] I. Lerner Publications Company. Geography Dept. II. Series: Visual geography series (Minneapolis, Minn.)
DS554.3.C345 1996
959.6—dc20
                                    95–37200

International Standard Book Number: 0–8225–1905–4
Library of Congress Catalog Card Number: 95–37200

## VISUAL GEOGRAPHY SERIES®

**Publisher**
Harry Jonas Lerner
**Senior Editor**
Mary M. Rodgers
**Editors**
Lori Coleman
Colleen Sexton
Joan Freese
**Photo Researcher**
Beth Johnson
**Consultants/Contributors**
David Wright
Douglas Pike
Sandra K. Davis
**Designer**
Jim Simondet
**Cartographer**
Carol F. Barrett
**Indexer**
Sylvia Timian
**Production Manager**
Gary J. Hansen

Photo © Dan Gair

**A mother in Phnom Penh holds her child. About 45 percent of Cambodia's population is under the age of 15.**

**Acknowledgments**

Title page photo © Nevada Wier.

Elevation contours adapted from *The Times Atlas of the World,* seventh comprehensive edition (New York: Times Books, 1985.)

1 2 3 4 5 6 – JR – 01 00 99 98 97 96

Photo © Dan Gair

Boys from Siem Reap, a town in northwestern Cambodia, play in a nearby river. This country's abundant water resources provide citizens with a means of irrigation and a source of fish.

# Contents

**Introduction** . . . . . . . . . . . . . . . . . . . . . . . . . . . . . . . . . . . . . . . . . . . **7**

**1) The Land** . . . . . . . . . . . . . . . . . . . . . . . . . . . . . . . . . . . . . . . . **10**
Topography. Water System. Climate. Flora and Fauna. Natural Resources. Cities.

**2) History and Government** . . . . . . . . . . . . . . . . . . . . . . . . . . . . **20**
The First Kingdoms. Angkor. Occupation and Civil Strife. French Colonization. 1930s to 1950s. War in Southeast Asia. Democratic Kampuchea. The Vietnamese Invasion. Recent Events. Government.

**3) The People** . . . . . . . . . . . . . . . . . . . . . . . . . . . . . . . . . . . . . **39**
Ethnic Groups. Family and Village Life. Religion. Education and Health. Language and Literature. The Arts. Festivals and Holidays. Food.

**4) The Economy** . . . . . . . . . . . . . . . . . . . . . . . . . . . . . . . . . . . **51**
Agriculture. Forestry and Fishing. Transportation and Tourism. Manufacturing and Foreign Trade. Energy and Mining. The Future.

**Index** . . . . . . . . . . . . . . . . . . . . . . . . . . . . . . . . . . . . . . . . . . . **64**

THAILAND

LAOS

SIEM REAP

KHONE FALLS

ANGKOR (Ruins)
● Siem Reap

Sangker R.

Tonle Sap

● Battambang

BATTAMBANG

Mekong R.

Tonle Sap R.

● Kompong Cham

KOMPONG CHAM

VIETNAM

● Oudongk

⊛ PHNOM
PENH

Bassac R.

● Kompong
Som

Kep

MEKONG
DELTA

Gulf of Thailand

SOUTH CHINA SEA

## CAMBODIA

N
↑

- - - - Province Boundaries

———— Major Roads

0          50          100  Miles

0     50     100  Kilometers

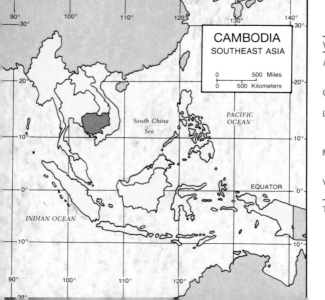

90°  100°  110°  120°  130°  140°
30°                              30°

## CAMBODIA
SOUTHEAST ASIA

0     500  Miles

0     500  Kilometers

20°                              20°

PACIFIC
OCEAN

South China
Sea

10°                              10°

EQUATOR

0°

INDIAN OCEAN

10°                              10°

90°
100°  110°  120°

## METRIC CONVERSION CHART
To Find Approximate Equivalents

| WHEN YOU KNOW: | MULTIPLY BY: | TO FIND: |
| --- | --- | --- |
| **AREA** | | |
| acres | 0.41 | hectares |
| square miles | 2.59 | square kilometers |
| **CAPACITY** | | |
| gallons | 3.79 | liters |
| **LENGTH** | | |
| feet | 30.48 | centimeters |
| yards | 0.91 | meters |
| miles | 1.61 | kilometers |
| **MASS** (weight) | | |
| pounds | 0.45 | kilograms |
| tons | 0.91 | metric tons |
| **VOLUME** | | |
| cubic yards | 0.77 | cubic meters |
| **TEMPERATURE** | | |
| degrees Fahrenheit | 0.56 (*after* subtracting 32) | degrees Celsius |

Family members thresh rice to separate the grain from the rest of the plant. Although three out of four Cambodians work in agriculture, the nation has been unable to produce enough to feed its own population.

# Introduction

A small, mostly rural nation of 10.4 million people, Cambodia lies on the southern portion of the Indochinese Peninsula in Southeast Asia. One of the poorest nations in the region, Cambodia is struggling to recover from years of war and famine.

The Khmer, the country's largest ethnic group, arrived from southern China more than 2,000 years ago. These settlers built villages and farms on a level, well-watered plain in central Cambodia, where rice cultivation became the basis of their economy.

The first large, organized state in what is now Cambodia was Funan, which arose in the first century A.D. Traders sailing from India brought new political systems, art forms, and religious practices to Funan. Khmer civilization reached its peak in the ninth century, when Khmer kings ruled a powerful empire centered in the vast city of Angkor. During the Angkor period, Khmer authority and culture spread into neighboring Laos, Thailand, and Vietnam.

The Khmer Empire began to decline in the fourteenth century, as hostile neighbors overran Angkor's government and temples. Newcomers such as the Cham and the Vietnamese began settling in Khmer territory in the fifteenth century. Overshadowed by the powerful realms of the Thai and the Vietnamese, Cambodia continued to shrink in size and importance until it became part of French Indochina in 1863. Seeking a trade route into China, the French neglected Cambodia after discovering that large ships could not navigate the Mekong River, Cambodia's principal waterway. After occupation by Japan during World War II (1939–1945), Cambodia won its independence peacefully in 1953.

Norodom Sihanouk served as the Cambodian king from 1941 to 1955 and as the nation's head of state from 1960 to 1970. During the latter period, Cambodia did not take sides while a war between Communists and non-Communists raged in Vietnam.

Norodom Sihanouk, Cambodia's king, has served as the nation's leader several times since he was first appointed king in 1941.

Photo © Luke Golobitsh

Cambodian students take a break from class at the teacher-training school in Kompong Cham, a city northeast of Phnom Penh. Cambodia is seriously lacking in educated teachers, a problem that must be resolved before the nation's school system can improve.

But in 1970, members of the Cambodian military seized power from Sihanouk. Cambodian Communists, known as the Khmer Rouge, overran the capital of Phnom Penh in 1975 and took over the government, heightening a civil war that would affect Cambodia for years to come.

Under their leader, Pol Pot, the Khmer Rouge forced people to leave Cambodia's cities and to live in rural work camps and farming collectives (government-owned estates). Two million Cambodian citizens were executed, died of starvation, or fled the country. To protect Vietnamese interests in Cambodia, Vietnam invaded in 1978 and installed a pro-Vietnamese government to replace the Khmer Rouge. Under international pressure, Vietnam withdrew its troops in 1989.

In 1993 elections supervised by the United Nations (UN) brought to power two political parties—Sihanouk's party and a Communist party run by officials of the former Vietnamese-led government. Sihanouk's party won the election, and Sihanouk was once again crowned king. With little money or resources, however, the party failed to take control of Cambodia's legislature. In the mid-1990s, Khmer Rouge troops were still fighting government forces in isolated regions of the country.

Despite continued warfare and the withdrawal of UN forces in 1994, Cambodians remain hopeful for a self-sufficient future. Throughout the country, people are rebuilding schools, repairing damaged homes and farmlands, and going back to work. With many thousands of Cambodians returning from exile, this age-old nation looks forward to developing a unified society and a strong economy.

9

Residents of a floating village on the Tonle Sap, a vast lake in central Cambodia, set off in canoelike boats. The lake provides abundant catches of fish for many Cambodians.

# 1) The Land

Roughly circular in shape, Cambodia is on the Indochinese Peninsula in Southeast Asia. The country's neighbors include Thailand to the west and northwest, Laos to the north, and Vietnam to the east and southeast. With a total land area of 70,238 square miles, Cambodia is about the size of the state of North Dakota. The country's greatest distance from north to south is 280 miles. From east to west, Cambodia stretches 360 miles.

## Topography

The major physical features of Cambodia are the Tonle Sap—a freshwater lake in central Cambodia—and the Mekong River, which flows southward through the eastern half of the country. A rugged, 200-mile coastline in southwestern Cambodia faces the Gulf of Thailand, an arm of the South China Sea.

A large, flat basin surrounds the Tonle Sap ("Great Lake" in Khmer, the official language of Cambodia). A network of artificial canals crisscrosses this basin, which contains fertile sediments left by seasonal flooding. The area is home to 85 percent of the country's population, most of whom cultivate rice in the rich soil. Hills ring the basin on all sides except the southeast. At this spot, the Mekong River, the largest waterway in Southeast Asia, branches into a wide delta (a low, wet plain at a river's mouth).

Surrounding the central basin are forests and highland regions. To the north are the Dangrek Mountains, which form steep sandstone cliffs along Cambodia's border with Thailand. The mountains and high plains that lie to the east of the Mekong River cross into southern Laos and Vietnam. In the southwest, the Elephant Mountains and the Cardamom Mountains separate the Tonle Sap basin from a coastal lowland that runs along the Gulf of Thailand. Cambodia's highest peak—Phnom Aoral—reaches an elevation of 5,949 feet in the sparsely populated Cardamom range.

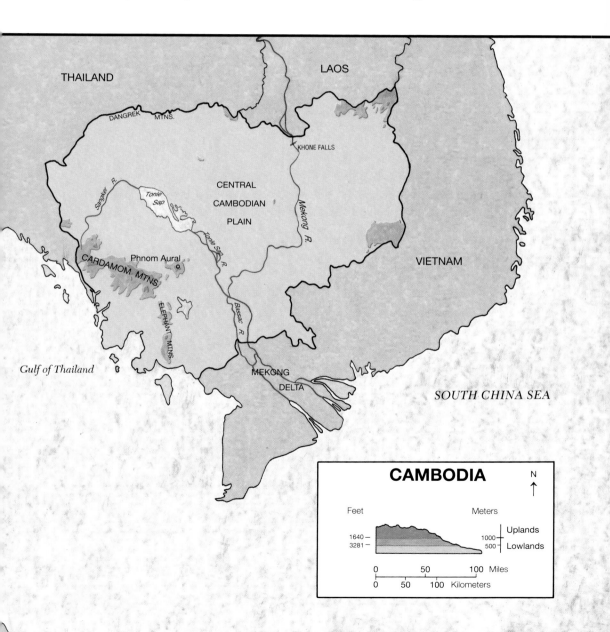

## Water System

Cambodia's major waterway is the Mekong River, which begins far to the northwest in the mountains of Tibet. Khone Falls marks the point on the Laotian border where the Mekong enters Cambodia. Carrying vast amounts of fertile soil downstream, the Mekong gradually widens before dividing into two branches at Phnom Penh.

Strengthened by the Tonle Sap, a river of the same name flowing south from the lake, the two branches of the Mekong continue into Vietnam. The lower branch, called the Bassac River, runs through southeastern Cambodia and southern Vietnam, emptying into the South China Sea. The upper branch splits into six smaller waterways before reaching Vietnam's seacoast.

For centuries Cambodia's rice farmers have used a complex system of earthen dikes and canals to divert the Mekong's waters to their fields. Besides providing water and soil, the river is an important source of freshwater fish, which Cambodians also net from the Tonle Sap, the Tonle Sap River, and the Bassac River. In recent years, aquaculture, or fish farming, has become an important economic activity along the Mekong, where families raise catfish and other species in artificial ponds.

A boater guides his watercraft down the Mekong River near Phnom Penh.

Some residents of the Tonle Sap area set up holding ponds in the lake to raise fish, including perch, smelt, and carp.

During the annual rainy season, the flooded Mekong may grow to a width of 20 miles. The rising level of the river forces its waters to back up into the 65-mile-long Tonle Sap River. This backup of water causes the lake to grow in size from 1,200 square miles to more than 3,000 square miles, creating a huge natural reservoir that can reach a depth of 35 feet. In the dry season, the Tonle Sap River drains the reservoir and again flows downstream into the Mekong. Along the Mekong itself, low water levels reveal rocks that lie in the river's bed, and dangerous rapids make boat travel up the river impossible.

## Climate

Cambodia's tropical climate is always hot and usually humid and rainy. From May through October, rain-bearing winds known as monsoons blow from the southwest across Southeast Asia, bringing moisture from the Indian Ocean. The southern coast of Cambodia—the wettest part of the country—receives 100 inches or more of rain each year, most of it during the summer monsoon.

Another monsoon wind coming from the northeast blows during winter, from November to March. But these milder winds from the South China Sea bring less moisture than the summer monsoons, and much of it falls as rain on northern Vietnam before reaching Cambodia. As a result, the winter months in Cambodia are drier than the summer season. In some years, the dry season stretches on for months without rain, leaving the terrain brown and cracked.

Average temperatures in Cambodia vary by only a few degrees throughout the year. Readings rarely fall below 70° F in low-lying areas or below 50° F in the highlands. The hottest months of the year are March and April. In Phnom Penh, the temperature averages about 80° F year-round. Rainy, destructive storms known as typhoons occasionally rake Southeast Asia. These storms often hit Vietnam's coastal areas hard and then diminish before reaching Cambodia.

## Flora and Fauna

At one time more than 70 percent forested, Cambodia had lost more than half of its woodlands by the late 1900s. Broadleaf evergreens still cover the highest hills and

Photo © John Elk III

A heliconia plant brightens the lush forest around Siem Reap.

Photo © Gerry Ellis/Ellis Nature Photography

A white-handed gibbon hangs from a tree in Cambodia. The smallest in the ape family, gibbons have no tails and rarely venture down from their treetop homes.

mountains of the north, while pines and deciduous (leaf-shedding) trees grow in other hilly areas. Thick tropical rain forests exist at lower elevations, where loggers harvest trees for lumber and for firewood. In 1993 and again in 1995, the Cambodian government banned lumber exports to control the rapid harvest of trees, which has occurred without efforts to replant. Illegal logging and lumber sales continue to deplete the country's remaining forests, however.

Marshes with tall grasses and reeds cover much of the central Cambodian plain. Surrounding highlands support prairie grasses. Along Cambodia's coast grow tangled mangroves, vines, rattans, palms, bamboos, and other woody plants. Cambodians harvest wild breadfruits, jackfruits, mangoes,

14

mangosteens, papayas, rambutans, and bananas for food. The durian is a strong-smelling, softball-sized fruit whose soft, sweet flesh is popular all over southeastern Asia.

Cambodia's mountains, plains, and forests are home to a variety of animal life. Tigers, bears, panthers, wild oxen, deer, and small monkeys live in sparsely populated regions. Asian elephants survive in the rural north and northeast. But the depletion of the country's forests has sharply reduced the numbers of these animals. Herons, cranes, pelicans, cormorants, egrets, and wild ducks flock to Cambodia's wetlands, while grouse, pheasants, and peacocks take refuge in the prairie grasslands.

The country also has many species of snakes, several of which—including the king cobra and the Russell's viper—are poi-sonous. The gecko, a small lizard, lives in or near many Cambodian homes, devouring insects but seldom bothering humans.

Cambodia has hundreds of varieties of saltwater and freshwater fish. Catfish larger than an adult human swim alongside carp, lungfish, and perch in the Mekong River. Fishers net tiny smelt from small waterways, as well as edible frogs, freshwater prawns (shrimp), and turtles.

## Natural Resources

With few natural resources besides the fertile soil brought downstream by the Mekong, Cambodians historically have relied on agriculture to earn a living. The most heavily farmed regions are the Tonle Sap basin and the major river valleys, which have been planted with rice for centuries.

Photo © Konrad Wothe/Ellis Nature Photography

**Asian elephants inhabit the rugged forests of Cambodia's remote border regions. Although the elephant population has fallen sharply in the twentieth century, experts estimate that about 2,000 of these majestic animals still live in Cambodia.**

Once considered Cambodia's most promising natural resource, the country's forests are in serious decline. Logging companies continue to harvest timber intensively with little supervision or control and no reforestation efforts. But logging has not yet affected areas that are difficult to reach because of rough terrain, lack of roads, and the presence of land mines left over from the civil war.

Deposits of iron ore, manganese ore, and gold exist in central and northern Cambodia, although the country's poor transportation network has prevented the development of these resources. Limestone quarries (excavation sites) in southern Cambodia provide an important building material, and Cambodia processes phosphate deposits into fertilizer for farm crops. Rubies, sapphires, and other precious stones are mined commercially in the western part of the country.

Cambodia imports nearly all of the energy it uses. But the country's rivers have enormous hydropower potential, and development of this resource is under way. Oil and gas deposits have been located in the South China Sea, where drilling is expected to yield substantial reserves. This discovery may help boost Cambodia's economy.

## Cities

Most Cambodians live in small, rural villages or on farms. Less than 13 percent of the 10.4 million Cambodians have homes in cities. Only Phnom Penh, Battambang, Siem Reap, and Kompong Som have more than 10,000 people. The populations of these cities fluctuated greatly during the wartime years of the 1970s and 1980s, reaching a low point during the reign of the Khmer Rouge. Urban populations have since begun to recover.

Lying in southeastern Cambodia, Phnom Penh (population 812,484) sprawls along the banks of three rivers—the Mekong, the Tonle Sap, and the Bassac. Cambodia's capital and largest city, Phnom Penh first developed in the 1400s as a river port, with an outlet to the South China Sea through Vietnam. Phnom Penh became the capital of Cambodia in 1867.

Workers unload wood at the Phnom Penh railway station. Once covered with thick woodlands, Cambodia has suffered serious deforestation in recent years. Timber is the primary building material, the main fuel, and a source of foreign income for many Cambodians.

Photo © Sarah Murray/The Hutchison Library

**Phnom Penh** *(above)* **has slowly recovered from years of warfare. By the mid-1990s, the city had become a stable capital with a growing economy. Its well-kept residential neighborhoods** *(below)* **are expanding on the city's outskirts.**

During the conflicts of the 1970s and 1980s, Cambodia's capital underwent drastic changes. In 1975 the Khmer Rouge evacuated the city and left its buildings to decay in the hot, humid climate. With the Vietnamese invasion and the arrival of UN peacekeepers in the 1980s, Phnom Penh saw the construction of new hotels and the reoccupation of abandoned homes and office buildings. The city's revival has since attracted foreign investors seeking low-cost labor for their manufacturing operations.

Foreign-aid organizations have contributed to the rebuilding of Phnom Penh, and tourism in the city is also bringing in foreign income that Cambodia can use to invest in the capital's development. Numerous dance clubs, a municipal theater, and a fine-arts school have opened since the end of the war. Although Phnom Penh is once again a bustling urban center, some of the city's people still suffer from poverty and unhealthy living conditions.

Battambang, the second largest city in Cambodia, has about 100,000 inhabitants. Located in western Cambodia, the city lies on the Sangker River about halfway between the Tonle Sap and the Thai border. Established as early as the tenth century, Battambang became part of Siam (modern Thailand) in the late 1700s. The city rejoined Cambodia in the early 1900s.

Battambang is served by a national highway and by the railway that runs from Thailand to Phnom Penh, 180 miles to the southeast. An active trading hub, Battambang has also been an important transfer point for sawed logs and other goods that are traded between Cambodia and Thailand. The city also is a starting

Photo by Matthew J. Petersen

**UN trucks parked on the streets of Battambang in the early 1990s.**

Photo © Nevada Wier

The Grand Hotel beckons visitors in Siem Reap, whose economy is based on tourism. The community lies near the ruins of Angkor, the ancient Khmer (Cambodian) capital.

point for tourists exploring ruins in the area. These ruins, such as the ancient monuments of Angkor, are considered among the world's outstanding architectural achievements.

In the northwest, close to Angkor, is the town of Siem Reap. Many of its 10,000 residents support themselves through tourism. Hotels and guide services assist visitors to the temples and monuments of Angkor. Street-market vendors offer souvenirs from Angkor, including rubbings of images laid in the stone temples and replicas of ancient musical instruments, crossbows, and knives.

Kompong Som, on the Gulf of Thailand, is Cambodia's only ocean port. This small city of 16,000 inhabitants lies about 130 miles south of Phnom Penh. Near Kompong Som is the seaside village of Kep. Once a pleasant and popular resort, Kep was destroyed by the Khmer Rouge in the 1970s. Plans to rebuild the town are under way.

Photo by Matthew J. Petersen

Cambodia's coastal region is sparsely populated, with few communities outside Kompong Som, the nation's only port.

A statue in Phnom Penh depicts an ancient mythical bird. Cambodian legends describe mountain peoples as descendants of Garuda, a divine bird, and river peoples as descendants of Naga, a divine fish or serpent.

# 2) History and Government

Archaeologists have found tools, pots, and other artifacts at many ancient sites in Cambodia. Although the country has been inhabited for at least 6,000 years, the identity of the earliest settlers is unknown. They may have been Australoids—people who migrated northward over time from Australia to southwestern Cambodia. These early peoples settled near the Tonle Sap and along the Mekong River. They relied on a diet of fish and lived in wooden houses raised above the surrounding marshy land.

Indonesians and islanders from the South Pacific region of Melanesia later moved into what is now Cambodia. These groups may have been fleeing enemies, searching for better hunting grounds, or looking to raise crops and livestock in more fertile fields and pastures.

By about 200 B.C., the Khmer—the ancestors of modern Cambodians—had migrated from the north into the Mekong River Delta. During the first century A.D., people were fashioning metal implements and weapons and bronze urns. This early economy was based primarily on fishing and on rice cultivation, making the Khmer one of the first groups to develop productive rice crops.

## The First Kingdoms

The Khmer established the kingdom of Funan nearly 2,000 years ago. Funan extended northward into what is now Vietnam, west into present-day Cambodia, and south along the Malay Peninsula (which includes part of modern Malaysia). The kingdom's capital, Vyadhapura, was located in southeastern Cambodia. Most of the realm's population lived along the Mekong and the Tonle Sap rivers. These waterways provided fish as well as plentiful water for the large-scale irrigation of rice, which some farmers could harvest as many as three times a year.

Through trade contacts, ancient Indian civilizations had a strong influence on the culture of Funan. Arriving from the west, Indian ships stopped in the kingdom's ports to take on fresh food and water. Indian traders, who followed the Buddhist or Hindu faiths, exchanged silk, iron, and bronze goods for valuable spices, gold, and ivory from the Indochinese Peninsula. Many of these Indian traders settled permanently in Funan, spreading Indian forms of government, art, and religion among upper-class Khmer.

By the third century A.D., Funan was powerful enough to command tribute

Photo © Nelson-Atkins Museum

An ancient sculpture depicts a standing Buddha. Buddhism spread to Cambodia from India, where the religion was founded in the sixth century B.C.

(payment) from smaller kingdoms in Southeast Asia. Funan also profited from trade between ports in the Indian Ocean to the west and ports on the Gulf of Thailand to the east. The kingdom's rulers collected surplus harvests of rice—as well as taxes in the form of jewelry, perfume, and precious metals—to pay for new construction projects. A small, wealthy upper class enjoyed privileges unknown to the large population of commoners, who worked long hours for meager earnings.

Continued trade and immigration from India strengthened the influence of Indian culture within Funan. Chandan, an Indian aristocrat, assumed the throne of Funan in A.D. 357. His successors used Sanskrit, an ancient Indian language, to spread Buddhism and Hinduism among the Khmer. Funan also adopted an Indian code of laws. Under King Kaundinya Jayavarman, who

ruled around the year 500, Funan reached the height of its power.

Despite the kingdom's wealth, life was short and harsh for most of its people. Ethnic minorities such as the Mon—tribal peoples in the northern highlands—were often forced into slavery. Many commoners suffered from easily spread diseases, including malaria, tuberculosis, and typhus, for which doctors had no cures. Food poisoning and deadly snakebites occurred frequently.

### CHENLA

In the seventh century, Chenla, a vassal (tribute-paying) state to the north of Funan, revolted against the kingdom. Under the rulers Isanavarman I and Jayavarman I, Chenla took control of Funan and expanded the new kingdom's territory.

Photo by North Wind Picture Archives

Settlements in Funan, an early kingdom centered in Cambodia, often clustered around lakes or along rivers. These locations provided water for irrigation, fish to eat, and convenient transportation links.

Photo © Nevada Wier

Yasovarman, a ninth-century ruler of the Khmer kingdom, raised the temple of Lolei in the ninth century. He was following a tradition established by Jayavarman II, an earlier king who had built temples to symbolize his authority.

In the eighth century, Chenla split in half. Upper (or Land) Chenla spread along the upper Mekong River through northern Cambodia and Laos. Lower (or Water) Chenla was based along the Mekong River Delta, reaching into modern Vietnam. Water Chenla suffered civil strife as well as sea attacks by people from the Malay Peninsula and from the kingdom of Sumatra (based in modern Indonesia). Eventually, parts of Water Chenla came under Sumatran control. At the same time, many small, independent Khmer kingdoms rose and fell in the remote plains and highlands of Southeast Asia.

## Angkor

In one of these kingdoms, the Khmer king Jayavarman II assumed control of the throne in 802 and set out to unify the Khmer peoples in Southeast Asia.

Jayavarman established a single Khmer state known as Kambuja (later Cambodia), named for the mythical founder of the Khmer people. A fervent follower of Hinduism, Jayavarman II established the cult of the god-king, which would remain popular for centuries.

Late in the ninth century, after Jayavarman II's death, his successors founded a new city, where they began building large, intricately designed monuments to honor the powerful empire that Jayavarman had established. An elaborate complex of stone temples, the city of Angkor instilled respect and fear among the neighbors of the Khmer, who saw the monuments as a sign of growing Khmer power. After becoming the capital of Kambuja around the year 900, Angkor grew as successive kings built additional temple complexes.

In the tenth and eleventh centuries, these Khmer kings pushed westward into

In the 1100s, Suryavarman II ordered the construction of Angkor Wat, the largest and the most fantastic of the temples at Angkor. The wat's many famous sculptures—which remain well preserved—feature monkeys, demons, beautiful dancers, and holy men and also represent ancient Indian tales and stories of Suryavarman in battle.

Thailand and built a sophisticated irrigation system. The new reservoirs and canals allowed Khmer farmers to produce large surpluses of rice, which in turn made Kambuja one of the most prosperous states in the region.

The kings of Kambuja commanded absolute obedience from their subjects. Laws required Khmer commoners to serve time in the king's military and to labor on temples, palaces, and irrigation projects. The Angkor civilization also supported a large class of wealthy landowners, whose job of managing rice cultivation was made much easier with a highly developed irrigation system.

Khmer administrative jobs were filled by a class of hereditary Hindu priests called Brahmans, who advised the king.

Several Brahmans acquired so much power that, around the year 1000, they had temples built to salute their glory. Although royal families mainly practiced Hinduism, both this religion and Mahayana Buddhism were observed in Kambuja. Some citizens also remained faithful to local religions, worshiping ancestors and spirits.

### UNREST AND CONFLICT

Suryavarman I, who reigned in the eleventh century, extended the realm of Kambuja farther westward into Thailand and eastward into Vietnam. But as the kingdom grew larger, it became more difficult to manage. Revolts broke out against heavy taxes, which were levied to pay for the capital's temples and monuments.

Members of several royal families vied for power, while Thai and Burmese forces threatened the western borders of the Khmer state.

Early in the twelfth century, King Suryavarman II defeated rival states in Vietnam and Myanmar. He also oversaw the building of Angkor Wat, a vast temple complex in the capital that is still the world's largest religious structure. But internal conflicts again weakened the kingdom after Suryavarman's death in 1150.

Champa, a small state on the Vietnamese coast, took advantage of the strife to rebel against the Khmer rulers. A Champa army invaded Kambuja and overran the Angkor region in 1177. A few years later, a Khmer prince named Jayavarman invaded and sacked Champa and proclaimed himself the new king of Kambuja.

Unlike previous kings, Jayavarman practiced Mahayana Buddhism instead of adopting the cult of the Hindu god-king. After assuming the throne as Jayavarman VII, he raised a great number of new temples, statues, and other public structures featuring Buddhas, gods, and kings. Inscriptions on the new monuments at Angkor described Jayavarman's success in extending the Khmer Empire westward into Vietnam, northward into parts of Laos and Thailand, and southwestward onto the Malay Peninsula.

### THE FALL OF ANGKOR

Before the end of Jayavarman VII's reign, however, the Angkor civilization began to disintegrate. Theravada Buddhism, introduced from Sri Lanka (an island nation off the southeastern coast of India), was based on simple devotion to the original teachings of the Indian philosopher, the Buddha. Unlike Mahayana Buddhism, Theravada Buddhism did not

A sculpted head stares out from a gateway at Ta Prohm, a temple built near Angkor Thom by Jayavarman VII. The king raised this and several other Buddhist shrines as monuments to close family members.

support the building of lavish temples to glorify the semimythical Khmer rulers.

As Angkor experienced religious change, Thai forces pushed the Khmer out of the central Thai valley and continued eastward into present-day Cambodia. Thai armies captured Angkor in 1353 and again in 1431, marking the end of the Angkor era. As Theravada Buddhism—also practiced by the Thai—became more popular, the Khmer abandoned Angkor and built a new capital to the south, on the site of modern Phnom Penh.

From their new location closer to the ocean and to trade routes, the Khmer came in contact with traders from China, Europe, and the Middle East. In the 1500s, the Khmer king Ang Chan moved the empire's capital to Lovek, north of Phnom Penh. Thriving trade in Lovek attracted settlers from China, Japan, the Malay Peninsula, Japan, the Middle East, and the European countries of Spain and Portugal. Merchants in the city bought and sold silk, cotton, ivory, precious stones, incense, and livestock.

## Occupation and Civil Strife

The sixteenth century was a time of disorder within Cambodia. Thai and Vietnamese armies occupied Cambodian territory, and Khmer rulers fought among themselves for power. To help his cause, a Khmer king named Sattha recruited soldiers from Spain, which sought land in Southeast Asia. But by the time the Spaniards arrived in 1594, Thai forces had already captured Lovek.

During the 1500s, European merchants braved the stormy waters of the South China Sea to stop in Khmer territory to trade their goods. The arrival of foreign powers in Southeast Asia eventually led to the region being colonized. The French took over Cambodia.

Thai misrule caused Cambodia to decline. Khmer leaders were forced to ally with either the Thai or the Vietnamese to retain land and power. As a result, foreign rulers gradually came to dominate Cambodian society.

While the Thai threatened the Khmer from the west, the Vietnamese approached from the east. After conquering Champa, Vietnamese forces pushed southwestward to the Mekong River Delta, which was populated by Khmer farmers. Around 1620 the Khmer king Chey Chettha allied with the Vietnamese. In return the Vietnamese demanded the right to settle in the Mekong River Delta. Vietnamese administrators took control of trade and agriculture in the region. By the late 1700s, the Mekong River Delta was completely under Vietnamese control, and the Khmer lost access to the sea.

Meanwhile, the Thai kingdom still threatened Cambodia from the west. After recovering from a defeat at the hands of the Burmese in 1767, the Thai established the new kingdom of Siam. This realm annexed (took over) several northern Cambodian provinces and also seized the provinces of Battambang and Siem Reap.

In the early nineteenth century, Vietnam and Siam again fought for control of Cambodian territory. After the death of the Khmer king Ang Chan II in 1835, the Vietnamese placed a young princess, Mei, on the Cambodian throne. Six years later, Chan's brother Ang Duong led a popular rebellion against Vietnamese rule. Fighting among Cambodians, Vietnamese, and Siamese continued for several years, until Cambodia agreed to be ruled jointly by its two neighbors. In 1848 the rival powers named Ang Duong as the new Cambodian king.

Although the Thai and the Vietnamese both ruled Cambodia with little concern for the Khmer population, their relationships with the Khmer differed greatly. The Thai shared with the Khmer a common religion and other aspects of culture such as literature. The Vietnamese, however, saw

Photo by Bettmann Archive

Opposition to French occupation and growing feelings of nationalism in the late 1800s sparked a renewed interest in traditional arts, including ancient Khmer dance.

the Khmer as a backward people who needed to be civilized.

## French Colonization

Tensions with Vietnam prompted Duong to negotiate with France, a European colonial power in Southeast Asia. The king's goal was to regain the Cambodian lands that had long been occupied by the Vietnamese. French colonial leaders wanted to slow the expansion of Siam, which had allied with Britain—France's European rival. The French government also sought to open a trade route along the Mekong River into China.

In 1863 the French persuaded the new Cambodian king, Norodom, to sign a treaty allowing France to exploit the kingdom's mineral and forest resources. In return the French agreed to protect the king against the Thai and against rebellions in his own realm. Under pressure Norodom signed another agreement in 1887 that

**27**

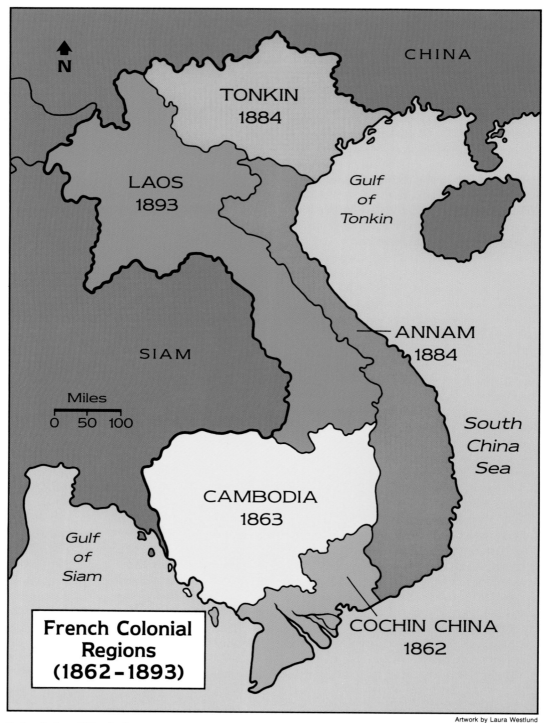

**N**

CHINA

TONKIN
1884

LAOS
1893

*Gulf
of
Tonkin*

SIAM

— ANNAM
1884

Miles
0   50   100

*South
China
Sea*

CAMBODIA
1863

*Gulf
of
Siam*

**French Colonial
Regions
(1862–1893)**

COCHIN CHINA
1862

Artwork by Laura Westlund

During the late 1800s, the French government expanded its influence in Southeast Asia, which includes modern Vietnam, Laos, Cambodia, and Thailand (then called Siam). Cambodia became a French protectorate in 1863. In 1887 France established the Indochinese Union—a French colony made up of Cambodia and the Vietnamese regions of Tonkin, Annam, and Cochin China. (Laos was added in 1893.)

transformed Cambodia into a French colony. The agreement abolished Cambodia's agricultural system, in which landless peasants were forced to work on the holdings of wealthy landowners. Under the French system, poor farmers had to take out loans to pay for land and were charged huge interest rates on the loans. In addition, the system levied large tax increases on the peasants. Khmer resentment of French control over Cambodian affairs steadily rose.

Relations between Norodom and the French colonizers grew increasingly strained. The French angered the king by allowing Siam to keep Battambang and Siem Reap, which the Thai had seized in the 1700s. As the French military presence in Cambodia expanded, France's control over the country increased, while the Cambodian monarchy weakened. Many of Norodom's rivals in Cambodia allied with the French to gain an advantage in their pursuit of power. In 1897 the French took over the Cambodian government, and the French resident general in Phnom Penh assumed authority over all domestic policy.

In 1904 King Norodom died and was succeeded by his half-brother, Sisowath. An old man when he became king, Sisowath cooperated with the French and ruled peacefully for more than 20 years. During his reign, French negotiators convinced Siam to return Battambang and Siem Reap to Cambodia.

During the 1920s, Cambodians built new roads and a railroad line. The French administrators established rubber plantations in eastern Cambodia and also began restoring the long-neglected temples of

Photo © John Elk III

**The Franco-Siamese Treaty Memorial in Phnom Penh commemorates a treaty that France and Siam signed in 1907. Under the treaty's terms, Siam returned Siem Reap and Battambang provinces to Cambodia, then a part of French Indochina.**

Angkor. Cambodia benefited from an expanding world market for rice, rubber, and corn. Although opposition to French rule weakened as the economy improved, the colonial labor system made virtual slaves of many Cambodian farmers. In 1927 the Cambodian military put down a protest over the labor system and over taxes.

## 1930s to 1950s

During the 1930s, the rising military power of Japan—an island nation to the northeast of Cambodia—was threatening many parts of Asia. During World War II (1939–1945), Japan joined the Axis alliance—which also included Germany and Italy—and fought against the Allied powers of Britain, France, the United States, and the Soviet Union. Although the Japanese overran Southeast Asia in 1940, the Japanese government allowed the French to administer the region. In 1941, however, Japanese leaders forced the French to cede Battambang and Siem Reap to Thailand (formerly Siam).

When the Cambodian king Monivong died in 1941, the colonial administrators placed on the throne Norodom Sihanouk—the grandson of King Monivong. Although the prince's father still lived, French officials believed they could more easily control the young man. But Sihanouk was an energetic and ambitious ruler who enjoyed widespread popularity among ordinary Cambodians. He sought to free Cambodia from foreign control and looked for an opportunity to fight for Cambodia's independence from France.

Sihanouk's chance came on March 9, 1945, when the Japanese government dissolved the French administration in Cambodia. Three days later, the king declared Cambodia's independence. But later that year, Japan was forced to surrender to the Allied forces, and Cambodia's colonial administration returned to power.

### THE STRUGGLE FOR INDEPENDENCE

After the war, Battambang and Siem Reap again were returned to Cambodia. Because France did not have the money or the troops to maintain control over the provinces, Siem Reap and Battambang were declared autonomous zones and enjoyed relative freedom from colonial authority. Meanwhile, the brief period of independence experienced in 1945 inspired many Cambodians to press for permanent self-rule. In 1946 France agreed to the formation of political parties and to

The newly crowned king Norodom Sihanouk attends the funeral of his grandfather King Monivong in 1941. Only 19 years old at the time, Sihanouk inherited a troubled nation.

French-led soldiers fire on Vietnamese troops in northern Vietnam. From 1946 to 1954, the French military fought Vietnamese forces for control of the government in Vietnam. In 1953, when France began losing ground in the war, the French government agreed to grant independence to the nations that formed French Indochina.

an election for an assembly, which would draft a national constitution.

Cambodian politicians formed two political parties—the Democrats and the slightly pro-French Liberals. The Democrats won a majority in the election and wrote a constitution. The document gave political power to the national assembly and left the king as a constitutional monarch, whose role in the government remained unclear.

The new national assembly lacked experience. In addition, members of the ruling Democratic party struggled with one another and with the king for power. Gov-ernment officials also disagreed about Cambodia's relationship with France. By 1953 King Sihanouk had dissolved the national assembly and had assumed power over the government.

France, however, still levied taxes, influenced foreign policy making, held sway over the judicial system, and maintained military bases in Cambodia. Still pressing for the country's full independence, Sihanouk left Cambodia in 1953, vowing to return only when the country was completely self-governing. He eventually settled in the autonomous province of Siem Reap, where he discussed Cambodia's independence with Lon Nol, the region's military commander. Later that year, the French formally granted Cambodia its independence, and Sihanouk returned to Phnom Penh.

Seeking to broaden his base of power, Sihanouk gave up the throne to his aging father and became a private citizen—an action that allowed him to run for political office. Sihanouk formed a new political party known as the Sangkum, which won every seat in the Cambodian legislature in 1955. As the party's leader, he became Cambodia's prime minister. In 1960, after the death of his father, Sihanouk declared himself the new Cambodian head of state.

## War in Southeast Asia

Meanwhile, Communist guerrillas, who favored single-party Communist rule, were fighting to topple the newly independent governments in Southeast Asia. By the 1960s, Vietnam was divided. A Communist government took charge in the north, supported by the People's Republic of China, a Communist country. A non-Communist government maintained control in the south with the help of the United States. A Communist guerrilla army based in the south and known as the Viet Cong began stepping up attacks on the South Vietnamese government.

As Cambodia's prime minister, Sihanouk tried to maintain a neutral foreign policy that balanced the interests of Communist and non-Communist powers. He feared the United States, an ally of both Thailand and South Vietnam, Cambodia's longstanding enemies. He also mistrusted the North Vietnamese, who were supporting Communist guerrillas in Cambodia.

In 1965, after the U.S. government began sending troops to South Vietnam, Sihanouk broke off relations with the United States and allowed North Vietnamese Communist (or Viet Minh) forces and the Viet Cong to station troops within Cambodia. Cambodian officials led by

General Lon Nol protested this policy. They favored ties with the United States and strongly opposed any negotiation with the Communists. When Lon Nol was elected prime minister in 1966, Sihanouk began losing influence.

With the aid of the United States, Lon Nol overthrew Sihanouk in March 1970.

President Lon Nol reviews Cambodian troops during a military ceremony. After his successful coup d'état (takeover) in 1970, Lon Nol remained in office until 1975, when the Khmer Rouge ousted him. Lon Nol's government promoted ties to the United States, which was helping South Vietnam wage war against North Vietnam, where Communists were in power.

North Vietnamese soldiers caught in Cambodia in the 1970s were often arrested by U.S. troops and taken to South Vietnam. During the Lon Nol era, Viet Minh and Viet Cong soldiers used parts of eastern Cambodia for military bases and supply routes. Committed to stopping the spread of Communism in Southeast Asia, the United States bombed the Cambodian supply lines.

Although initially popular, Lon Nol lost the trust of the people when his army began killing ethnic Vietnamese in Cambodia. At the same time, U.S. forces began bombing eastern Cambodia, where the Viet Cong had built bases and supply routes.

The Lon Nol government also failed to reverse the effects of a faltering economy. While government officials enjoyed prosperity, average Cambodian villagers lived in poverty. As fighting spread throughout Cambodia, food production in the country fell sharply. Food shortages, rising prices, and the high costs of the war further damaged Cambodia's economy.

After losing control of the government, Norodom Sihanouk took refuge in China, where he worked to overthrow Lon Nol by forming the National United Front of Cambodia and by rallying for international support. Meanwhile, young Cambodians

studying in France had been organizing Communist political groups for years. During the 1960s, they took control of the Cambodian Communist movement, now known as the Khmer Rouge (Red Cambodians). As they moved through the Cambodian countryside in the early 1970s, Khmer Rouge troops encouraged young villagers to join the movement. With the Cambodian economy in ruins and opposition to the Lon Nol government growing, many Cambodians took up arms with the Communists.

Under the leadership of a former schoolteacher named Pol Pot, the Khmer Rouge waged war against the better-equipped but poorly motivated Cambodian armed forces. The Khmer Rouge received some assistance from the Viet Minh and the Viet Cong, who were gaining the upper hand in South Vietnam.

A woman mourns the destruction of her village in eastern Cambodia in 1973. In that year, the U.S. Army launched a major bombing assault on the region in an attempt to destroy Communist forces.

Photo by UPI/Bettmann

In 1974 the Khmer Rouge overran the city of Oudongk north of Phnom Penh, forcing out the city's 20,000 citizens. Teachers, government employees, and other intellectuals were murdered. In the spring of 1975, the Khmer Rouge closed in on the capital of Phnom Penh. The guerrillas captured the city on April 17, in the same month that South Vietnam fell to North Vietnam.

## Democratic Kampuchea

Many Cambodians who initially supported the Khmer Rouge believed that political ties existed between the Communist movement and Sihanouk, who remained popular. Although Lon Nol's government had been corrupt and unpopular, the Khmer Rouge regime was far worse. The new leaders renamed the country Democratic Kampuchea and established one of the most brutal governments in Cambodia's history.

In the mid-1970s, the Khmer Rouge evacuated Phnom Penh and other cities and sent urban residents to forced-labor camps in the Cambodian countryside. In the deserted cities, markets were closed, the monetary system was abolished, and mail delivery ceased. Even rural Cambodians lost their land and were forced to work in the fields for the Khmer Rouge, although many were allowed to stay in their villages. In addition, the Khmer Rouge arrested and executed teachers, intellectuals, journalists, artists, and anyone associated with the Lon Nol government.

Exhausted from backbreaking labor, many Cambodians died of starvation, disease, and overwork. Executions and torture were routine. Children were taken from their parents at the age of seven, housed in children's units, and taught the Khmer Rouge philosophy. Malay, Vietnamese, and other ethnic minorities in Cambodia suffered as much as the ethnic Khmer. Anyone able to escape left the country.

Many different factions existed within the Khmer Rouge. But Pol Pot, who became prime minister in 1976, was the undisputed leader of the country. He and a few other Khmer Rouge officials were hostile toward the Vietnamese government, which they feared could undermine Cambodia's independence. Pol Pot and his allies purged the Cambodian government, executing any official who did not share their anti-Vietnamese sentiments.

The Khmer Rouge continued to attack minority groups in Cambodia, particularly Vietnamese living near the Cambodia-Vietnam border. By 1977 the Khmer Rouge army was invading Vietnamese territory, an act which eventually led to open warfare between the two nations.

Meanwhile the Khmer Rouge invited Norodom Sihanouk to return to Phnom Penh as the head of state. He was later detained by the Khmer Rouge after resigning in protest of the government's brutality. Sihanouk was placed under arrest in the royal palace for several years. Eventually he was able to escape and again flee Cambodia.

Photo © Dan Gair

A painting in the Tuol Sieng War Museum in Phnom Penh documents some of the terrible offenses carried out by the Khmer Rouge in the 1970s. After taking power in 1975, the Khmer Rouge set up a strict and brutal regime.

Attacks on ethnic Vietnamese in Cambodia prompted Vietnam to invade Cambodia in 1978. Vietnamese forces found piles of bodies in locations throughout the country, where the Khmer Rouge had set up prisons and execution centers.

## The Vietnamese Invasion

In December 1978, Vietnam invaded Cambodia. The Cambodian people had little motivation to defend the Khmer Rouge regime. The Vietnamese quickly captured Phnom Penh and set up a pro-Vietnamese government called the People's Republic of Kampuchea (PRK). The PRK, made up largely of pro-Vietnamese Communists who had deserted the Khmer Rouge in the late 1970s, forced Pol Pot and his supporters into exile along the Thai border.

The new PRK regime reopened Cambodia's schools and hospitals, permitted city dwellers to return to their homes, and allowed some forms of trade. But these measures could not rescue the country's economy. Rice production remained low, and Cambodia had to rely on foreign aid for food. Much of the food aid, however, was smuggled into Vietnam or confiscated by the Cambodian government.

Meanwhile, thousands of Cambodian refugees opposed to the Vietnamese occupation fled to Thailand. Citizens who remained in Cambodia were forced to join the PRK army and were imprisoned for seeking freedom from Vietnamese control. In remote areas of the Cambodian countryside, forces allied with the Khmer Rouge, with Norodom Sihanouk, and with the former Lon Nol government fought among themselves and against the PRK for control of Cambodia.

Between one and four million people—or at least 15 percent of Cambodia's total population—died under the Khmer Rouge regime. Hundreds of thousands more fled Cambodia after the Vietnamese invasion. In the 1980s, the government of Vietnam uprooted more than one million of its citizens and moved them into Cambodia to colonize the country. This action resulted in cultural clashes and in concern among the ethnic Khmer about losing their own identity. These concerns led to an even greater desire for self-rule among Cambodians.

## Recent Events

An international economic boycott of Vietnam forced the Vietnamese government to withdraw its troops from Cambodia in 1989. New political parties formed in the country. They ranged from the anti-Communist Khmer People's National Liberation Front (FNLKP) to Norodom Sihanouk's National United Front for an Independent, Neutral, Peaceful, and Cooperative Cambodia (FUNCINPEC). Later Sihanouk left the leadership of this party to his son, Prince Norodom Ranariddh.

In 1991 the Vietnamese-backed government agreed to step down in favor of multiparty elections. By this time, Cambodia had four main political groups—the FNLKP, which included many supporters of the former Lon Nol government; FUNCINPEC; the state-run Cambodian People's party (CPP); and the Party of Democratic Kampuchea (PDK) led by Communist Khmer Rouge leaders. The four groups agreed to a peace settlement and began negotiations to set up a new government.

In 1992 the United Nations (UN), an international diplomatic organization, sent peacekeeping forces and administrators to oversee elections, held in 1993. The PDK boycotted the vote, which FUNCINPEC won. FUNCINPEC gained a majority in the assembly, which adopted a parliamentary monarchy and elected Sihanouk as Cambodia's king. The CPP and two smaller parties also won seats in the assembly. Because CPP leaders had run the previous Cambodian government, that party retained much control over the new coalition govenment. CPP officials fought to maintain authority over the government's administrative and judicial functions so the party could use funds and interpret laws as it saw fit.

As the Cambodian government faltered through the mid-1990s, the Khmer Rouge continued to oppose the new regime from guerrilla bases established in the Cambodian countryside. Khmer Rouge leaders have maintained control over small areas across the country and are recruiting young villagers who are desperate to escape rural poverty. Although the Khmer

Peacekeepers sent by the United Nations arrived in Cambodia in 1992—after Vietnam had pulled out and after several political parties had begun vying for power. Besides overseeing the 1993 elections, the UN operation was committed to guaranteeing civil rights and to disarming opposing factions.

Photo © Dan Gair

Rouge has lost its allies in China and other nations, Thai military leaders continue to provide the guerrillas with arms, financial support, and a safe base in Thailand. In return, the Khmer Rouge supplies the Thai with lumber and precious gems smuggled from Cambodia.

Weakened by corrupt officials and political infighting, the Cambodian government has been unable to control the Khmer Rouge. Moreover, some governmental leaders and military officers have been involved in arms sales to the guerrillas and in other illegal activities. Meanwhile, political instability is only one of the country's major problems. Cambodia's economy continues to falter as prices remain high and food is scarce—problems the government has failed to address.

## Government

In September 1993, Cambodia's national assembly adopted a new constitution, which formally established a new national government. The government, a parliamentary monarchy, has a king, two co–prime ministers, an advisory council, and a legislature. Cambodia's legislature, the National Assembly, has 120 elected members. Eighteen ministries have responsibility for different governmental tasks, and the heads of each ministry sit on the Council of Ministers, the prime ministers' cabinet.

Cambodia's 1993 constitution also set up a new judicial system made up of a supreme council of judges and a constitutional council. Appointed by the king, members of the supreme council include judges, prosecutors, and other judicial personnel. The constitutional council has nine members—three appointed by the king, three appointed by the president of the National Assembly, and three named by the supreme council of judges. The constitutional council reviews laws and approves those it finds to be constitutional. Under these two councils is a local judicial system made up of court judges, lawyers, and law-enforcement officials.

The red and blue Cambodian flag, adopted in 1989, features Angkor Wat, a symbol of Khmer culture at its peak. The red stripe represents the defense of the Khmer homeland and the struggle of the Khmer people for prosperity and peace. The blue stripe stands for national unity and the wealth of the country.

Artwork by Laura Westlund

Cambodian refugees travel from a refugee camp in Thailand back to their homes in Phnom Penh. About 370,000 Cambodians returned in the early 1990s. Most had left Cambodia to escape Khmer Rouge brutality or to flee the invading Vietnamese.

# 3) The People

Although there has been no official census in Cambodia since the early 1960s, current estimates put the population at 10.4 million. Civil war, the uprooting of urban families, and emigration have all taken their toll on Cambodian society. In addition, hundreds of thousands of Cambodians fled to refugee camps in Thailand during the periods of Khmer Rouge and Vietnamese rule. Many of these refugees later resettled in other countries. By May 1993, the UN had repatriated (sent back) approximately 330,000 Cambodian refugees.

Cambodia is sparsely populated, with an overall density of about 155 persons per square mile. Because parts of the nation are poorly watered or hard to reach, the population is concentrated in the central basin and plains and in the lowlands near the Mekong River. Isolated highlands in the north and tropical rain forests along the coast have the country's lowest population densities.

## Ethnic Groups

Ethnic Khmer began settling in Southeast Asia more than 2,000 years ago. Over the centuries, several other groups moved into Cambodia. Traders and merchants

**39**

Some ethnic Vietnamese in Cambodia live in floating villages on the Tonle Sap and its adjoining river. The nation's Vietnamese population of about 400,000 was a main target of Khmer Rouge attacks in the early 1990s.

Photo © Wolfgang Kaehler

from India, for example, began arriving in the eighth century A.D. The Thai formed an important class of immigrants to Cambodia from the tenth to fifteenth centuries. Cham peoples—from the ancient kingdom of Champa in what is now Vietnam—emigrated after their defeat by the Vietnamese in the 1400s. Vietnamese people came in the seventeenth century, and ethnic Chinese migrated to Cambodia in the eighteenth and nineteenth centuries.

After taking power in 1975, the government of Democratic Kampuchea worked to expel minority groups. As a result, the Khmer now make up about 96 percent of the population, and Cambodia has become the most ethnically uniform nation in Southeast Asia. Nevertheless, several ethnic minorities have survived.

Most ethnic Chinese still live in the cities, where for centuries they have played an important role as merchants and traders. Vietnamese farmers live in rural areas of eastern Cambodia. The Cham, most of whom follow the Islamic religion, reside in small villages throughout Cambodia.

The Khmer Loeu, or highland people, are a group made up of many tribes related to the earliest inhabitants of Southeast Asia. They live mainly in the isolated hilly and mountainous areas of northeastern Cambodia. Many Khmer Loeu practice slash-and-burn agriculture, in which a section of rain forest is felled and burned to provide fertile land for growing crops. When the land can no longer support crops, the inhabitants move on to a different area.

## Family and Village Life

As the upheavals of civil war have eased, many Cambodians are returning to their traditional way of life. In most households, parents live together with their children, who remain in the home until they marry. Grown children take in aging parents who can no longer care for themselves.

About 87 percent of Cambodians live in rural areas. Most Cambodian villages stretch along a road, a river, or a canal. A street market, a few shops, a school, and a Buddhist temple are central to the village. Shops are made of stucco or cement, but many of the houses and schools are constructed of palm thatch and bamboo. More prosperous villagers have wood houses with roofs of tin or other metal. Small gardens, fruit and shade trees, and bushes adorn village homes.

Most farm families leave their village each morning after breakfast to plant, weed, or harvest in nearby rice paddies. The laborers return home at noon to eat the largest meal of the day and then rest during the hottest midafternoon hours. After working in the fields in the late afternoon, they prepare dinner.

Village adults typically wear a *sampot,* a knee-length garment that hangs loosely from the shoulders. T-shirts, military-style shirts or pants, shorts, and either tennis shoes or rubber sandals are also common. Many Cambodian men and women favor a traditional red-and-white checkered scarf known as a *krama,* which protects them from the sun's intense rays.

## Religion

The vast majority of Cambodians follow Buddhism. This faith traces its origins to an Indian prince named Siddhartha Gautama, who lived around 500 B.C. Weary of his privileged life, Gautama embraced spirituality and practiced fasting and meditation. Through right actions and thought, he believed a person could overcome desire, which he saw as the root of the world's suffering. He described an eightfold path to reach nirvana—a state of being that is without desire and suffering. After reaching nirvana, Gautama took the name Buddha, meaning Enlightened One.

Cambodians practice Theravada Buddhism, one of the two main branches of Buddhism. Theravada Buddhism tries to limit Buddhist doctrines to the teachings of the Buddha. Mahayana Buddhism, the form practiced in China and elsewhere, adopts the writings of others and emphasizes the existence of many buddhas.

Buddhism in Cambodia centers around the village wat, or temple, where Buddhist monks live and worship. Temples have no regularly scheduled services, but monks play a vital role in the lives of average Cambodians. These religious leaders

Many Cambodians wear traditional clothing, which includes the *krama (left)*. Others, especially young people *(right),* prefer jeans and T-shirts.

A Buddhist monk waits to perform a wedding ceremony in a small Cambodian village. More than 90 percent of the Cambodian population follow Theravada Buddhism, but many Buddhists also include elements of Hinduism and other faiths in their worship.

participate in all festivals as well as in weddings, funerals, and other ceremonies. In the morning, the monks leave the temple and walk along the street, accepting offerings of food from the villagers. Monks spend much of their time meditating but also teach school and counsel villagers.

Every male Buddhist is expected to become a monk for at least a short period of time after he finishes school and before he marries. The usual time served is about three months, but a few novices choose to remain monks for part or all of their adult life. Females may become nuns, but most do not until they are older. Many of these nuns are widows, who also live in the wat and carry out specific tasks, such as preparing the altar and housekeeping.

Several other major religions are practiced in Cambodia. Until the fourteenth century, Hinduism existed side by side with Buddhism. Angkor, built in the ninth century, was named for a Hindu god. In modern times, the number of Hindu sects in Cambodia has declined. The Cham are Muslims—followers of Islam, a religion founded in the Middle East. They and a

few Malay Muslims worship in mosques (Islamic houses of prayer). Ethnic Chinese residents of Cambodia may follow Mahayana Buddhism mixed with different types of ancestor worship. Respect for ancestors also is important among most ethnic Vietnamese, some of whom are Buddhists and others of whom follow the Roman Catholic faith that the French brought to Southeast Asia. The religion of Cao Dai, a mix of Christian and other beliefs, also has a small number of Vietnamese supporters. In contrast, the Khmer Loeu peoples practice animism— the worship of spirits believed to be present in natural objects such as rocks and trees.

## Education and Health

Besides serving religious needs, monks in village temples traditionally have provided an education to Cambodian youth. In urban areas, state-run schools have also been established. But many families need their children to help with labor-intensive farmwork and do not send youngsters to school. As a result, the literacy rate in Cambodia is about 38 percent, a low figure compared to the rest of Southeast Asia.

Education suffered greatly under the Khmer Rouge, which closed schools and executed many of Cambodia's teachers. Most people who grew up during the Khmer Rouge period are illiterate. Although the PRK government reopened schools and training centers, education remained limited or unavailable to many Cambodians because of shortages of teachers, books, equipment, and money.

In the early 1990s, about 1.3 million students were enrolled in Cambodian primary schools. But about 50 percent of primary-school students drop out, and, of those who complete their courses, only about 35 percent go on to secondary school. Estimates report between 200,000 and 300,000 youth enrolled in secondary schools in Cambodia. A small university and a technical school offer postsecondary education in Phnom Penh, but few Cambodian students have the necessary educational backgrounds to enter postsecondary schools. Wealthy Cambodians who can afford it send their children out of the country for their education.

Health services in Cambodia are unable to keep pace with the many tropical diseases that still rage throughout the country. Even nonfatal ailments, such as dengue fever, can leave the victim very weak for days. Malaria, an illness carried by mosquitoes, affects a large percentage of the population, and the water throughout Cambodia contains typhus and other harmful bacteria. Cambodia's

Photo © Wolfgang Kaehler

Young students play in their school courtyard in Siem Reap. The lack of funds earmarked for education in Cambodia continued to hinder educational development in the mid-1990s.

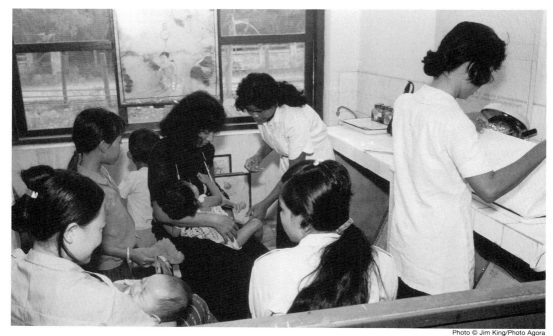

Women, some with small infants, wait for routine checkups in a Cambodian maternity clinic. Cambodia has few medical professionals, with an average of about 60 doctors and about 450 nurses per every one million people in the population.

few hospitals remain too poorly equipped to treat patients with serious health problems, and prescription drugs are very hard to find. Consequently, folk medicines are popular, even though their rate of effectiveness varies.

Unsanitary conditions and poor nutrition also contribute to the health problems of Cambodians, whose average life expectancy is only 50. (The average rate for the rest of Southeast Asia is 64.) Infant mortality—the number of babies who die before their first birthday—stands at 108 out of every 1000 live births—the highest rate in the region.

## Language and Literature

Cambodia's official language is Khmer, whose unique alphabet is based on an ancient Indian script. The spoken language has 33 consonants and many vowels. The pronunciation of each consonant varies, according to the preceding or following vowel. Eight different consonants represent sounds that fall between the pronunciations of the English letters *t* and *d*.

From the late 1800s to the 1960s, French was an important second language in Cambodia. Although some older Cambodians still use this Latin-based tongue, an increasing number of Cambodians in international business speak English. Besides Khmer, Asian languages such as Malay, Vietnamese, and Cantonese (a Chinese dialect) are commonly heard in the capital.

Cambodia has a rich tradition of myth and legend based on the *Ramayana,* a Hindu epic that originated in India. Thai literature also has influenced Cambodian writers historically. More recently, Cambodians have developed their own novels, poetry, and theater and film scripts. These artistic forms of writing were banned during the Khmer Rouge regime, although recent efforts to rejuvenate Cambodian literature have had some success.

Signs in Phnom Penh advertise English language lessons. As more Cambodians gain a basic education, students grow more interested in second languages and in other specialized fields.

## The Arts

Cambodia's principal works of art and architecture belong to the temple complex of Angkor. Over a period of 500 years, skilled artists, craftspeople, and laborers raised Angkor's sculptures and structures, which have survived damage from seven centuries of heat, monsoon rains, neglect, and war. Angkor remains the largest religious shrine of any kind in Southeast Asia.

The temple monuments were based on Hindu teachings about politics, history, and religion. Each major temple served as the center of a royal cult. The temple highlighted a king's personality and achievements during his reign and served as a tomb at his death. Other temples were centers for other kinds of Hindu cults and feature a number of the Hindu gods carved in stone.

Bicyclists near Angkor transport woven baskets to the market in Siem Reap. Many artisans in the area sell their wares to tourists who come to visit the ruins.

More than 70 structures exist in the Angkor area. Represented on and around the monuments are dozens of gods, goddesses, angels, devils, armies, animals, and mythological beasts. The Terrace of Elephants, for example, features a 400-foot-long row of carved, life-sized elephants. Long after Angkor was abandoned, Khmer artists continued to make reproductions of these works in stone.

In 1986 archaeologists and engineers from India began efforts to restore the aging temples. The restoration team, along with hundreds of unskilled Cambodian workers, is scrubbing the monuments with chemicals, reassembling crumbled stone columns and arches, and filling cracks with cement. Some experts have criticized these restoration methods, which have rubbed off detailed carvings and have mismatched cement with the soft, delicate sandstone structures. These experts want to discontinue the cleaning and feel that only steps to prevent further damage should be taken.

Although an estimated 90 percent of all dancers died or were killed by the Khmer Rouge between 1975 and 1978, the traditional Cambodian art of *lamthon* dancing has survived. Lamthon dancers skillfully move their hands and bodies to strike graceful, dignified poses. In rural areas, troupes of dancers travel from village to village, performing dances as well as plays inspired by Hindu myths and folktales. Dancers also perform at Angkor, acting out legends from the Hindu epics. Orchestras accompanying the dancers feature drums,

Photo © Nevada Wier

Restoration workers clean and reconstruct the temple of Angkor Wat. Some of the structure's huge sandstone blocks have even been copied and replaced. Jungle overgrowth, settling, erosion, and warfare have damaged some of the ancient buildings at Angkor, prompting technicians to restore the temples and shrines.

gongs, flutes, xylophones, and one- and two-stringed violins.

Important Cambodian handicrafts include pottery, jewelry making, goldsmithing, and wood carving. Lacquerware is a popular craft common to Cambodia and its neighbors in Southeast Asia. To create a lacquered object, the artist covers a wooden surface with a hard, smooth, and shiny coating of tree resin.

Cambodian weavers transform silk and cotton into bright and long-lasting bolts of cloth. Virtually every village has makers of mats and baskets. Craftspeople often draw on religious or mythical themes in

A classical temple dancer *(left)* performs in Angkor Wat. Many Khmer dances mimic the dramatic and graceful forms of the sculpted figures featured on the walls of Angkor's monuments. Using traditional methods, a weaver *(below)* spins thread, which will then be woven into cloth.

An artist in a Phnom Penh factory paints a small sandstone statue of the Buddha, which will probably end up in a Cambodian home.

Photo © John Elk III

their works. Religious figures, particularly of the Buddha, are produced on charms and ornaments. Small figures carved from stone are also popular.

## Festivals and Holidays

Traditional Cambodian holidays usually follow the lunar (moon) calendar, which changes every year. As a result, the dates on which the events are celebrated may vary from one year to the next. Cambodians celebrate a variety of local and national religious and secular (nonreligious) holidays.

National festivals include Tet, the lunar New Year, which arrives in late January or early February. Celebrated primarily by Chinese and Vietnamese minorities, Tet is a time of family reunions, of repaying debts, and of starting the new year properly. Chaul Chnam, the Cambodian New Year, is a three-day celebration that takes place in mid-April. During Prachum Ben, in late September, Cambodians make offerings to their ancestors. In late October or early November, when the Tonle Sap again begins to flow into the Mekong River, a water festival occurs, with boat races in Phnom Penh.

Each year on November 9, Cambodians celebrate the independence they won from the French in 1953. On National Day in early January, Cambodians commemorate the overthrow of the Khmer Rouge by the Vietnamese in 1979. On May 9, Genocide Day, ceremonies mourn those who suffered at the hands of the Khmer Rouge.

## Food

Cambodian cuisine borrows many dishes from Thailand, Vietnam, Malaysia, and China. Despite the warm temperatures year-round, soup is popular, served only slightly warmed or even at room temperature. Cambodians prepare hot-sour fish soup, ginger-flavored pork soup, and prawn or shrimp soup.

A popular accompaniment to soup is fish, a staple food that Cambodians prepare several ways. It can be grilled, steamed, stuffed with dried shrimp, wrapped in lettuce or spinach leaves and dipped in sauce, or cooked with vegetables in a round steel wok. Coriander, lemongrass, and mint leaves flavor fish. These herbs also commonly appear in cold salads made of greens mixed with bits of beef, egg, and other items.

Cooks sometimes add chicken, pork, or beef to soups and fried-rice dishes. But for average Cambodians, meat is usually scarce. A single chicken, for example, will be spread over several meals, even when many mouths are being fed.

Cambodians also enjoy a variety of noodle dishes, including rice noodles cooked

Newlyweds and their family members take a stroll in Phnom Penh after the wedding ceremony.

Photo © Wolfgang Kaehler

in coconut milk. Chinese and Thai noodle dishes are popular throughout the country. When times are good, every meal includes rice, usually grown by those who consume it. Balls of sticky rice mixed with fresh banana are a favorite food for festivals and holidays. *Ansamcheks* are pressed rice cakes with banana filling.

Larger Cambodian cities have French bakeries that offer a variety of breads. Pastries made with palm sugar are fried and rolled in grated coconut. A popular pudding is made with jackfruit. Fruits and fruit dishes are common desserts. Drinks include many kinds of fruit juice, beer, rice whiskey, and soft drinks, but the most common and popular drink for any time of day is tea.

**Sweets** *(above)* **made of rice and coconut sit on display at a market in Wat Po village, near Siem Reap. Cambodian markets also feature a wide variety of fresh greens and other vegetables** *(right)*, **most of which are raised on small family farms.**

Photo © Wolfgang Kaehler

Photo © Jim King/Photo Agora

Cambodian farmers discuss plans for a rice irrigation project with an agricultural expert. Although agriculture employs most Cambodians, the nation continues to have to import food.

# 4) The Economy

Cambodia's economy has long been based on agriculture. Historically rice and rubber were the two principal exports, a situation that made the nation dependent on unpredictable markets and prices for these goods. Although rural families were largely self-sufficient in food production before the 1970s, civil war and the Khmer Rouge regime brought economic collapse and widespread famine to Cambodia. By the time Vietnamese forces withdrew in 1989, Cambodian cities and farms were still struggling to recover from these disasters.

The arrival of the UN mission in 1991 proved to be one of the most important events in Cambodia's recent history. Thousands of foreign troops and administrative staff arrived in the capital, greatly raising the demand for food, housing, and consumer goods. Cambodia's gross domestic product (GDP)—the total value of all goods

**51**

and services produced within the country in a year—rose by 13.5 percent in 1991 and by 8 percent the following year. A building boom took place in the capital, although foreign workers filled most of the jobs for skilled laborers. A flood of foreign consumer goods arrived, and vendors sold them in street markets and stalls to the members of the UN mission.

Cambodians who were elected to public office in the UN-sponsored national election in 1993 hoped to build a solid government and a growing economy. The UN withdrawal in 1994 allowed them to independently plan the nation's future. But the departure of UN employees also harmed many service businesses in and around Phnom Penh. Barbers, launderers, maids, bellhops, bartenders, and other workers lost customers. Food vendors saw an important market for their goods disappear. Real estate values declined, and so did prices of rental properties in the capital.

Although Cambodia still relies heavily on foreign aid, the nation's leaders hope to create a strong, self-reliant economic base. Donor nations, including Japan, France, and the United States, have pledged a total of $1 billion to the new government, with additional funds on the way from the World Bank and from the International Monetary Fund. Most Cambodians are desperately poor, with a GDP per person of only about $280 per year. With much of the damage and dislocation of war still affecting the economy in the 1990s, Cambodia has a long way to go to achieve self-sufficiency.

Refugees returning to Cambodia from Thai border camps in the early 1990s received supplies from UN personnel. Having lost all but the clothes on their backs, most refugees hoped to rebuild their villages and their lives.

A woman stoops to plant individual rice seedlings. Lacking tractors and other machinery, almost all Cambodian farmers plant and harvest their crops by hand.

## Agriculture

Cambodia's geographical features have hindered the growth of agriculture. Mountains, highlands, and areas with thick overgrowth leave a limited amount of land suitable for crops. In fact, only about 17 percent of Cambodia's total land area can be cultivated. Even in the central basin, the soils lack nutrients, and seasonal rainfall can be unpredictable. But as the overflow in the Tonle Sap drains each winter, the water leaves behind rich sediments in which rice can be grown.

Dependence on a single crop hits Cambodia hard in years when rice production

falls because of flooding or drought. In addition to the natural problems farmers face, many families cannot afford mechanized equipment and still plow with a pair of oxen or water buffalo.

By the mid-1990s, three out of every four Cambodians were working in the agricultural sector, which makes up more than three-fourths of the nation's GDP. The country has about 15 million acres of cropland and almost 4 million acres of pasture. But the ongoing conflict between Khmer Rouge troops and government soldiers has taken nearly one-third of Cambodia's available farmland out of production. In

**53**

addition, vast minefields laid during the civil war make large farming areas unsafe. In fact, experts estimate that at least 10 million mines remain buried throughout the Cambodian countryside.

Cambodia finally became self-sufficient in rice production in the 1960s, but the war that soon followed once again made the nation a food importer. Annual production of rice, Cambodia's main crop, hovered at about four million tons during the 1980s and early 1990s, even though more acreage was being planted. The yield per acre varies, depending on the availability of water pumps, plows, spare parts, and fertilizer. Government controls on the price of rice further discourage large harvests.

Other important food crops include potatoes, yams, cassavas, soybeans, mung beans, sesame seeds, groundnuts, and vegetables such as corn, cucumbers, and peppers. Fruits grown in Cambodia include bananas, coconuts, durians, mangoes, papayas, citrus fruits, and pineapples. Some farmers also raise poultry and hogs.

Rubber plantations cover about 20,000 acres, about half as many acres as were cul-

UN peacekeeping forces trained Cambodian military personnel to search for and defuse the millions of mines buried in the country.

A fisher on the Tonle Sap pulls in a heavy net. Although Cambodia's inland water system is extensively fished, little fishing takes place off the coast.

tivated in 1970. Each year workers collect the trees' latex, the raw material for making rubber. Almost all of Cambodia's production is exported, either as raw latex or as finished vehicle tires. The largest single plantation—the 5,000-acre Chup Plantation in Kompong Cham province in eastern Cambodia—employs 6,000 workers.

To improve rural development, the Cambodian government has ordered banks to reserve 10 to 20 percent of their capital for farm loans. In September 1994, the Japanese government granted $6 million to Cambodia for the purchase of fertilizers and agricultural equipment. Nevertheless, Cambodia's periodic droughts continue to harm production and cause famine. Recent droughts and flooding hit the northwest and the south. International relief agencies sent donations of food as well as mechanical water pumps to improve rice production in the region.

## Forestry and Fishing

Cambodia's forests are among the nation's most valuable natural resources. But uncontrolled harvesting of these trees is threatening the survival of Cambodian woodlands. Loggers cut an average of 120,000 acres of trees each year, and six provinces have been entirely cleared of wood. Continued guerrilla fighting has prevented any reforestation programs. The worst cases of illegal cutting take place along the Thai border, where loggers can quickly haul felled trees out of the country.

Surviving forests are important to the health of Cambodia's fishing industry. Trees hold down soil that otherwise washes into rivers and lakes. And by absorbing rainfall, forests prevent flooding, which can disrupt fish-breeding areas. As a result of large-scale forest clearing, Cambodian fishers have seen smaller fish harvests since 1990.

A UN transport plane sits outside the Phnom Penh airport, which bears a large painting of Norodom Sihanouk.

Most Cambodian farmers raise or catch fish to supplement their families' diet. The Tonle Sap and the Mekong, Bassac, and Tonle Sap rivers provide abundant catches of perch, lungfish, eels, carp, and smelt.

## Transportation and Tourism

Long-term warfare has prevented Cambodia from maintaining or improving its transportation system. Heavy seasonal flooding often blocks or damages roadways, and mines laid during the civil war are still a traveling hazard.

About 9,000 miles of roads, less than 2,000 of which are paved, cross Cambodia. Most of the country's 4,000 passenger cars and 7,000 trucks operate in and around Phnom Penh, although many city dwellers use bicycles or pedicabs (large tricycles equipped to carry passengers) for transport. In the countryside, most people travel by foot or oxcart. A trip by automobile or truck through remote areas can be halted by bandits, washed-out roads, weak or absent bridges, shortages of parts, and lack of fuel.

Numerous passenger ferries cross the Mekong River, while small oceangoing vessels sail upriver to Phnom Penh by way of Vietnam. Kompong Som, Cambodia's main port on the Gulf of Thailand, is linked to the capital by a four-lane highway.

Railways run from Phnom Penh to Battambang in the northeast and from the capital to Kompong Som on the coast. But explosive mines laid along the tracks frequently cause damage to railway cars as well as to crew and passengers.

Plans are under way to convert Phnom Penh's airport into a modern, international facility. Daily commercial air services carry travelers between Phnom Penh and Bangkok, Thailand, as well as on regular flights to Vietnam, Hong Kong, Malaysia, Singapore, and Laos. At least three domestic air services link Cambodia's major cities.

Using the airport system, foreigners travel to Cambodia's major tourist destination—the temple complex at Angkor. War and instability, however, have discouraged visits to this area for many years. By the mid-1990s, only a few thousand visitors were arriving annually. The lack of hotels, telephones, and other services, as well as a poor transportation network, have deterred people from making the trip.

A tourist approaches the entrance to Angkor Wat. Despite the threat of Khmer Rouge attacks, the number of travelers visiting Cambodia increased in the 1990s.

Photo by Reuters/Bettmann

Nevertheless, the number of tourists visiting Cambodia has substantially increased each year in the mid-1990s. To encourage tourism, the government has reduced the cost of foreign visas, which are usually only issued to people on organized tours. The majority of tourists fly into the country from Bangkok. Others arrive from Vietnam, which is also trying to encourage tourism.

## Manufacturing and Foreign Trade

Industry is a small sector of Cambodia's overall economy. The country lacks skilled laborers, spare parts, raw materials, and the foreign investment needed to build a strong manufacturing base. In the past, the government owned and controlled most manufacturing operations. Many state-owned facilities proved to be inefficient, however, and in the early 1990s, the

Photo © Timothy Beddow/The Hutchison Library

Phnom Penh's main marketplace bustles with activity. Cambodians hope for peace and stability, which would allow the economy to continue growing.

**57**

Cambodian government began selling these enterprises. Foreign developers—as well as Cambodians living abroad—have bought state enterprises and have modernized or converted them to other uses. Although some Cambodians have lost their jobs as a result, officials believe that foreign investment will improve industrial growth in the future.

By the end of 1994, about 70 privately owned factories were operating in Cambodia, most of them located in or near the capital and employing about 100 people each. The majority of these enterprises process the nation's agricultural products—timber, fish, rice, and rubber. Other plants produce household goods, cement, textiles, beer and soft drinks, cigarettes, nails, sacks and bags, automotive and bicycle tires, tools, and pharmaceuticals. Many of the plants operate below capacity, a problem brought on by shortages of raw materials. In addition, electrical power failures periodically slow or stop production.

A pharmacy in Siem Reap offers a wide variety of medicines and other remedies.

In Phnom Penh, a seamstress sews a colorful dress. As Cambodia's economy begins to improve, small businesses are starting to appear in the capital and other urban areas.

Photo © Nevada Wier

For many years, Cambodia has run a trade deficit, meaning the country imports more goods from foreign companies than it sells abroad. Cambodia's main imports are machinery, fuel, food, textiles, and electrical goods. The nation's principal exports are rubber, unprocessed timber, red corn, soybeans, sesame, and tobacco.

Cambodia's leading trading partners include its Southeast Asian neighbors, to which the country exports its agricultural goods. Cambodia imports manufactured items from Germany, Japan, the Netherlands, and the United States. A heavy trade in food and goods with Thailand occurs in areas controlled by the Khmer Rouge, outside government regulation and taxation. The smuggling of valuable lumber and gemstones also takes place from these areas.

Cambodian men chat outside a shop that sells small motors in Phnom Penh. Most machinery available in Cambodia is imported from foreign manufacturers.

Photo © John Elk III

Photo © Jim King/Photo Agora

A man gathers wood scraps to use for fuel. Firewood accounts for the majority of the fuel used in Cambodia.

## Energy and Mining

The principal source of energy in Cambodia is firewood, which is most commonly used for cooking or converted to charcoal for heating. The country's production of electricity tripled during the 1980s, from 60 million to 180 million kilowatt hours per year. Four electrical facilities operate in Phnom Penh, and Japan and the former Soviet Union constructed several other plants around the country.

The Soviet Union also supplied Cambodia with petroleum until 1991, when the UN arrived. Since then Singapore and Thailand have served as the country's principal petroleum suppliers. The Cambodian government leases offshore exploration rights to foreign oil and natural gas

drilling companies. In the future, the rivers of the northeast may offer sites for new hydroelectric dams. Hydropower could provide Cambodian homes and industries with a dependable domestic source of energy.

Cambodia has little mineral wealth. Deposits of iron ore, limestone, kaolin, silver, and tin exist but have not been mined commercially. A total of 10 separate deposits of gold have been discovered in Cambodia. In the mid-1990s, Australian, Malaysian, and Cambodian companies were planning gold-mining operations. The Khmer Rouge has set up an informal and illegal mining operation for gems—mostly sapphires and rubies—in the northeastern part of the country.

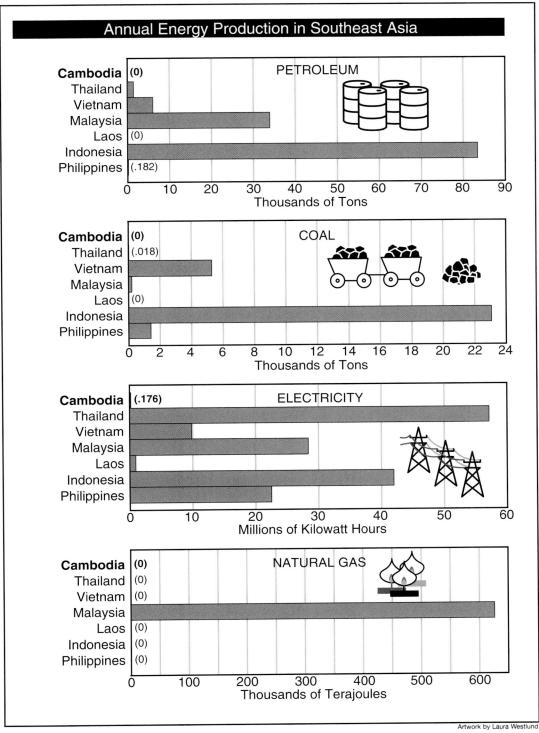

## Annual Energy Production in Southeast Asia

**PETROLEUM**

Cambodia (0)
Thailand
Vietnam
Malaysia
Laos (0)
Indonesia
Philippines (.182)

Thousands of Tons

**COAL**

Cambodia (0)
Thailand (.018)
Vietnam
Malaysia
Laos (0)
Indonesia
Philippines

Thousands of Tons

**ELECTRICITY**

Cambodia (.176)
Thailand
Vietnam
Malaysia
Laos
Indonesia
Philippines

Millions of Kilowatt Hours

**NATURAL GAS**

Cambodia (0)
Thailand (0)
Vietnam (0)
Malaysia
Laos (0)
Indonesia (0)
Philippines (0)

Thousands of Terajoules

Artwork by Laura Westlund

This chart shows energy production in Southeast Asia in the early 1990s. Cambodia will have to boost production to become economically competitive in the future. (Data from *Key Indicators of Developing Asian and Pacific Countries,* 1994.)

**61**

Urban development—such as this new building under construction in Phnom Penh—indicates that the Cambodian economy is growing after years of warfare and poverty.

## The Future

Compared to the grim recent past, the future may hold a better life for the Cambodian people. With development aid from Japan and other Asian countries, economic growth is likely to continue as new factories are established in the cities. Equally important goals—such as mapping and dismantling the country's many minefields—may foster the development of transportation, agriculture, and tourism.

In its struggle to establish a stable government, Cambodia's leaders must still contend with the Khmer Rouge guerrilla movement in the countryside and also with widespread corruption among government officials. Although the Khmer Rouge remain a threat, they have lost the support of China, a major source of money and arms. If the fragile political coalition now in power is able to settle differences with Thailand and Vietnam, to attack government corruption, and to develop the economy, Cambodia may at last be on the path toward peace, stability, and economic development.

Photo © Dan Gair

Children listen to their teacher in a classroom in Siem Reap. Cambodia's youth represent the nation's greatest hope for a peaceful and economically sound future.

# Index

Agriculture, 7, 15, 29–30, 40, 51, 53–55. *See also* Rice; Rubber
Ang Chan, 26
Ang Chang II, 27
Ang Duong, 27
Angkor, 7–8, 19, 23–26
  architecture of, 29–30, 42, 45–46, 56
Angkor Wat, 24–25, 38, 46–47, 57
Aquaculture. *See* Fish farming
Archaeological findings, 20
Architecture, 45
  restoration and construction of, 29–30, 46, 62
Arts, 45–48. *See also* Handicrafts
Australia, 20
Bassac River, 12, 16, 56
Battambang, 16, 18–19, 27, 29–30, 56
Brahmans, 24
Britain, 27, 30
Buddha, 25, 41
Buddhism, 21, 22, 41. *See also* Mahayana Buddhism; Theravada Buddhism
Cambodia
  boundaries, size, and location of, 10
  flag of, 38
  population of, 39
Cambodian People's party (CPP), 37
Cham, 8, 40, 42
Champa, 25, 27, 40
Chandan, 22
Chenla, 22–23
Chey Chettha, 27
China, 7–8, 26–27, 32, 37, 41, 49, 63
Chup Plantation, 55
Cities, 16–19. *See also* Battambang; Phnom Penh
Civil wars, 9, 26–27, 40, 51
Climate, 13–14
Clothing, 41
Colonization, 27–30
Communists, 8–9, 32–34, 36. *See also* Khmer Rouge
Constitution, 38
Democratic Kampuchea, 34–35, 40
Democrats, 31
Economy, 7, 38, 51–63
Education, 9, 42–43, 45, 63
Emigration, 39
Energy, 16, 60–61
Ethnic groups, 39–40. *See also* Cham; Khmer; Thai; Vietnamese
Exports, 14, 51, 55, 59
Family life, 40–41
Famine, 7, 51, 55
Fauna, 14–15
Festivals, 42, 48–49
Fish and fishing, 5, 10, 12–13, 15, 20, 21, 55–56
Fish farming, 12–13, 56
Flag, 38
Flora, 14–15
Food, 14–15, 49–50, 54
Foreign aid, 18, 36, 52, 55, 63
Foreign investment, 18, 55, 57–58
Foreign trade, 59

Forests and forestry, 16, 55
France, 27–31, 33, 52
Franco-Siamese Treaty Memorial, 29
French Indochina, 8, 28, 29, 31
Funan, 7, 21–22
Germany, 30, 59
Government, 38
Gross domestic product (GDP), 51–53
Guerrillas, 32, 34, 37–38, 55, 63
Handicrafts, 47
Health, 43–44
Hinduism, 21, 22–24, 42, 45, 46
History, 7–9, 20–38
  Angkor, 7–8, 19, 23–26
  archaeological findings, 20
  early kingdoms, 21–23
  French colonization, 27–30
  independence, 30–32
  recent, 37–38
  Vietnamese invasion, 36–37
  war, 32–35
Holidays, 48–49
Housing, 40–41
Hydropower, 16, 60–61
Imports, 16, 51, 54, 59
Independence, 8, 30–32, 49
India, 7, 21, 22, 25, 40, 44
Indian Ocean, 13, 22
Indochinese Peninsula, 7, 10, 21
Indonesians, 20
Industry, 57–59
Infant mortality, 44
International Monetary Fund, 52
Irrigation, 5, 21, 24, 51
Isanavarman I, 22
Italy, 30
Japan, 8, 26, 30, 52, 55, 59–60, 63
Jayavarman I, 22
Jayavarman II, 23
Jayavarman VII, 25
Jayavarman, Kaundinya, 22
Judicial system, 38
Kambuja, 23–25
Khmer, 19–27, 29, 38, 39–40, 44, 47
  empire, 7–8, 25
Khmer Loeu, 40, 42
Khmer People's National Liberation Front (FNLKP), 37
Khmer Rouge, 9, 16, 18–19, 33–38, 39, 40, 49, 59, 61, 63
  effects on Cambodia, 43–44, 46, 51, 53, 57
Khone Falls, 12
Kompong Cham, 9, 55
Kompong Som, 16, 19, 56
Lakes, 12–13. *See also* Tonle Sap (lake)
*Lamthon* dancing, 46–47
Land, 10–19
Language, 44–45
Laos, 7, 10–12, 23, 25, 28
Liberals, 31
Life expectancy, 44
Literacy, 43
Literature, 44
Logging, 14, 16, 55
Lon Nol, 32–36, 37
Lovek, 26
Mahayana Buddhism, 24–25, 41, 42

Malay Peninsula, 21, 23, 25–26
Manufacturing, 18, 57–59
Maps and charts, 6, 11, 28, 61
Mei, 27
Mekong River, 8, 10–13, 16, 23, 27, 39, 48
  fish from, 15, 20–21, 56
Mekong River Delta, 20, 23, 27
Melanesia, 20
Middle East, 26
Minefields, 54, 56, 63
Mining and minerals, 16, 61
Mon, 22
Mountains, 11
Myanmar, 25
National Assembly, 38
National resources, 15–16
National United Front for an Independent Neutral, Peaceful, and Cooperative Cambodia (FUNCINPEC), 37
National United Front of Cambodia, 33
Norodom, 27, 29
North Vietnam, 32–34
Oudongk, 34
Party of Democratic Kampuchea (PDK), 37
People, 39–50
  ethnic groups, 39–40
  festivals, 48–49
  literacy, 43
  village life, 40–41
People's Republic of Kampuchea (PRK), 36, 43
Phnom Aoral, 11
Phnom Penh, 16–18, 43, 48–49, 52, 59–60, 62
  history of, 9, 20, 26, 29, 32, 34–36
  temperatures in, 14
  tourism in, 56–57
Political parties, 9, 30–32, 37
Pol Pot, 9, 33, 35–36, 49
Population, 4, 7, 39
Poverty, 18, 33
Rainfall, 13–14
Rain forests, 14, 39–40
Ranariddh, Norodom, 37
Refugees, 39, 52
Religion, 25–26, 41–42. *See also* Buddhism; Hinduism
Rice, 7, 10, 12, 15, 20–22, 24, 30, 36, 41, 51, 53–54
  food prepared with, 49–50
Rivers, 5, 12–13, 16. *See also* Mekong River; Tonle Sap (river)
Roads and highways, 18, 56
Rubber, 51, 55, 59
Rubber plantations, 29–30, 54–55
Rural areas, 16, 40
Sangker River, 18
Sangkum, 32
Sattha, 26
Siam, 27–29. *See also* Thailand
Siem Reap, 16, 19, 27, 29–31
Sihanouk, Norodom, 8–9, 30–33, 34, 35–37, 56
Sisowath, 29
Slash-and-burn agriculture, 40
Slavery, 22

South China Sea, 10, 12–13, 16, 26
Southeast Asia, 7, 10–11, 13–14, 23, 26–28, 32–33
South Vietnam, 32–34
Soviet Union, 30, 60
Spain, 26
Sri Lanka, 25
Sumatra, 23
Suryavarman I, 24
Suryavarman II, 24, 25
Thai, 8, 25–27, 29, 38, 40, 44, 52, 55
Thailand, 7, 10–11, 49, 56, 63. *See also* Siam
  historical events in, 24–25, 30, 32
  refugee camps in, 36, 38, 39
  trade with Cambodia, 18, 59–60
Thailand, Gulf of, 10–11, 19, 22
Theravada Buddhism, 25–26, 41–42
Tibet, 12
Tonle Sap (lake), 10–13, 15, 18, 20, 40, 53, 55, 56
Tonle Sap (river), 12–13, 16, 21, 40, 48, 56
Topography, 10–11
Tourism, 18–19, 45, 56–57
Trade, 18, 26
Transportation, 18, 56
United Nations (UN), 9, 18, 37, 39, 51–52, 54, 60
United States, 30, 32–33, 34, 52, 59
Viet Cong, 32–33
Viet Minh, 32–33
Vietnam, 7–9, 10–12, 16, 49, 56–57, 63
  historical events in, 21, 23–25, 27–28, 31–37
Vietnamese, 8–9, 18, 26–27, 33, 35–37, 39–40, 42, 49
Village life, 40–41
Vyadhapura, 21
War, 7, 32–34, 51–52, 56. *See also* Civil wars
World Bank, 52
World War II, 8, 30